LESSONS LEARNED

As A Young African American Woman

In Information Technology

LAQUATA SUMTER

ACKNOWLEDGEMENTS

My 1st official book of many is dedicated to my grandparents Henry and Richerdina Sumter.

I would like to say a special thank you to my parents Albert and Georgiann(Dent) Sumter for being my cheerleaders always. Thank you to all those who have supported me over the years and continue to support me. A special thank you of support goes to my god mothers Patricia Dover & Monique Green, Spiritual Mothers Dr. Wendy R. Coleman & Rev. Gloria S. Brown, and my Aunt who is more like a mother to me Arlene Sumter.

TABLE OF CONTENTS

INTRODUCTION

I t is indeed a great opportunity and a huge blessing to be a Black Woman. However, what society thinks about black women can often lead to racism and gender discrimination, which is a cankerworm that has eaten deep into the world entirely. This could make black women think and feel less of ourselves, and though some people may believe that our skin is dirty or ugly, in actuality, our skin is highly rich in melanin, which protects our skin from the harmful effects of ultraviolet radiation.

Some black women sometimes think low of themselves and their abilities, mainly because they are a woman, but their race contributes to this thought as well. For a long time, and presently, black women have fallen at the end of the social spectrum of life.

Too, many beliefs and ideologies surround black women, with some that have been in place for centuries. One example is the thought that black women were meant to spend their whole life in the kitchen, attending to domestic chores and sitting in the house taking care of their family. This has led to many neglecting their passion, gifts, talents, and, most importantly, their education and certificates that lead to achievement.

Black women have suffered racism, limitations, and oppression because of their skin color and gender. Each of these things has instilled fear, caused pain, and has led to constraints that cannot easily be understood. Too, it can be challenging to see the benefits, gifts, and talents black women were born with and have developed in their life due to these consistent constraints, and the discouragement faced, because of our race and gender.

As black women, we should believe and prove to the world that we can not only thrive in our existence, but also make a significant impact in this world. These impacts could not only be in the field of home-keeping, but we have the high capacity to make a significant impact academically, industrially, socially, and economically. We can keep our homes, career, work, or businesses, all at the same time, because when it comes to multitasking, black women are the BOSS.

Now, irrespective of the severe damage negative assumptions of black women have caused, most black women have been able to rise and live above the hurt, and have become women that people look up to as role models. There are many black women out there doing things that are great and inspiring, and they live without concern for the negative beliefs, limitations, and societal discouragements that stem from race and gender discrimination. They believe in what they love, their passion, gifts, and talents.

It's obvious that black women are making positive and significant impacts in the world and are excelling in many different platforms, some within the fashion industry, entertainment industry, technical and engineering field, and in the business industry too.

Black women are not just ordinary women. They have within them great values, wisdom, beauty, inspirations, power, and strength. Each of these qualities enable them to stay strong, achieve whatever they want to achieve, and overcome any challenges they may face. Again, black women are not just ordinary women. Black women are superwomen, only without the capes.

A good lesson to learn is that research has shown that for black and white women employed in white-collar occupations, 22% of African American women aspire to be in a strong position with a magnificent title, compared to 8% of white women who have the same vision. So, step-up your aspirations, aim high, and be the best you can be, and this includes excelling at being a black businesswoman in the business world.

These are just a few reasons why it's excellent and also a huge blessing to be a black woman. One of the first steps to becoming a successful black woman is the total acceptance of who you truly are and to embrace your heritage. Don't let your education and certificates, dreams and aspirations, gifts and visions, and your talent, go down the drain because of some negative beliefs, gender inequality, or racism, as these count for nothing and amount to nothing too.

You are a black woman, yes you are, so be proud of who you are. Take a look into the mirror, and appreciate your black womanhood.

This book will help you get to the top of your game and will teach you useful steps that will make you and your business stand tall in many fields, to include: IT, engineering, and the business world. This book will also help you make your business known globally, while aiming to open your eyes to the many opportunities that are available in the business world and to understand how to access those opportunities.

You are not only endowed with beauty, a great body, and great skin, but also with a great and super brain to turn the world around for the better and make positive and significant changes. If you dream it or visualize it, then you can be it and do it.

As you flip through this wonderful, interesting, and educating book, I hope you gather and utilize the knowledge you gain. I can't wait to see you among the top black women CEOs, Engineers, IT Consultants, and Businesswomen of the world.

CHAPTER ONE
GAINING CERTIFICATIONS EARLY

Information Technology has shown a terrific growth rate since the inception of the industry and now stands with other giant sectors such as health and agriculture. Because it improves effectiveness and efficiency in virtually every other industrial area, Information Technology may even rate above every other industry.

Information Technology is usually divided into six main jobs, to include:

- Technical support
- Programmers
- Web developers
- Computer systems analyst
- IT security
- Network engineers

Each of these positions and offices are highly specialized and require specialized training to become proficient in them. Unsurprisingly, institutions offering courses in IT also provide a host of certifications based

LA QUATA SUMTER

on the specialization and operating fields. There are even certifications for persons who teach courses for the Information Technology field.

Studying for these certifications is not as hard as you might think or expect, and they are entirely worth it. Even at my start, I did not agree with my mentors until I got a chance to compare myself with my colleagues.

Some of the specialized certificates include:

Cisco Certified Network Associate (CCNA): being a lower-level certificate, it verifies an individual's capability and skill in installing, operating, and configuring enterprise-level switches and routers, and solving common systems and network problems.

CompTIA A+: an entry-level and a standard starting point for anyone hoping to build a career in Information Technology. Technicians with this certificate are verified to have skills in the maintenance of PCs, mobile devices, laptops, operating systems, and applications.

CompTIA Network+: globally acknowledged and validates an engineer's ability to design, manage, and troubleshoot both wired and wireless networks.

Certified Information Systems Security Professional (CISSP): globally recognized and validates an individual's capability in securing an organization from cybernetic attacks, while also pointing to extensive technical training and the managerial ability of an engineer to create and manage information security applications and programs.

Microsoft Certified Systems Engineer (MCSE): a mid-level certificate that confirms an individual's strength in the specialized areas of server infrastructure, enterprise devices and application, data platform, business intelligence, messaging, communication, private cloud, desktop infrastructure, and others.

Other certificates include the Microsoft Certified Trainer (MCT), Microsoft Certified Solutions Associate (MCSA), and more, but you get the idea.

In retrospect, gaining certifications early-on is one of the best things that has happened to me. However, at the time, I had no idea. I was more interested in hanging out with friends and lacked a definite plan for what I wanted to do with my life. These are a few things I learned by getting my certifications early.

Lessons Learned

Increases Your Chances and Value on the Labor Market

I have found that the more certifications one possesses, the more opportunities one will have, and when job seeking, having specialized certifications enables one to get into positions that would otherwise have been unavailable. There are very few people who have seen the advantages and necessities of acquiring a specialized certificate. This means that in any given group of job seekers, having an extra certificate would ensure that you gain an edge and stand out in the crowd. It also ensures that your job entry level is higher. Employers will tend to pay you better and provide you with more senior ranking position titles than if you didn't have an extra certificate. A certificate also informs your employer of your knowledge and abilities, and assures them of your skill level and proficiency in specific areas. This, therefore, definitely improves an employer's assessment of you and your potential contributions to their establishment.

I know many people will say that passing some exam does not mean that one is precisely capable when it comes to solving problems. Well, this may be true in some cases, and especially in cases where individuals only aim for certification to increase the abbreviations that occur after their names. Honestly, if you are this kind of person, I say good luck. Certificates can be used as bragging rights. For instance, imagine your name being called out at a social event: Ms. Bridgette BSC MSC CISSP MSCA blah, blah, blah, blah, and BLAH. I know, who am I to judge? It's just as important that you pursue certifications with the right mindset, and with the intent to learn more. The extra reading and research involved in passing the examinations ensures that you are rightfully exposed to situations that you would ordinarily not come across. It also ensures that you have extensive knowledge while improving skills that you may not be aware you needed or even understand.

You Have More Time to Invest

One very essential resource available to a young person is time. Due to the lesser number of responsibilities, as a younger woman, I had more attention to devote to study, classes, and research. Older friends, on the other hand, had to cope with relationships, children to care for, and a 'cheerful' boss at the office. I was able to make important advancements without having to deal with complications that may arise, especially those that related to pleasing a spouse or partner, maintaining a busy schedule, or dedicating time for focusing on research.

I do know, however, that this would have been a problem for me otherwise, as I am not very good at remembering to show my loved ones how much I care. As a young black woman trying to prove my ability and my value, it was sometimes easy to become more focused on studies and preparation for exams that I would forget everything else. This is a sure recipe for destroying a relationship. During that time, I did not appreciate the extent of development and growth I was achieving by sacrificing my free time. The time I would have spent hanging out with friends, spending time at the mall, losing sleep over social media trends, and hunting every movie in the theatres, could have taken away from my achievements. I understood that I had to break up some friendships, time spent with friends, and time spent on some activities, which had to all be reduced. However, there came a hidden bonus, as the friends who remained proved their loyalty and provided support when they discovered I had to improve myself. I also think that this new pursuit kept me so busy that I had no time to get into trouble with my parents or the police, which is a plus.

You Can Have Others Bear the Cost

Another hidden advantage to getting certifications at a younger age is that the funds and costs could mostly come from someone else. The cheapest exams for those certificates listed above cost about $200. Too, one would need to buy books, pay for online research materials (such as videos) and learning aids, transportation, and more. The list could go on and on. In this, having a job will help, and having a job with a sponsor as well would be that much better. Even more, having a very able sponsor is most preferred, but not everyone is that lucky. As a young lady, it was quite easy for me to acquire sponsorship, perhaps even easier than if I was older. My mentors were my number one go-to whenever I needed funds. Extended family members and former teachers would occasionally lend a hand when asked, as well. I know, too, that being older perhaps would have reduced the number of individuals I could reach out to for financial aid because these individuals may have labeled me as an adult and would have been looking up to me for financial assistance rather than understanding that I needed their help.

That being said, having a job would have only worked if I had registered part-time. Studying full-time with a job is not extremely stressful, but I would have run the risk of failing an exam and having to retake the paper. Yes, that's another exam fee, and it's time going down the drain. Even still, failing an exam as a youngster is not as bad as it would have been if I was older. The nagging mentors or parents would always be there to force me to try again. Whereas on my own, I probably would have given up and decided to try my hand at something else. The support of my mentors and parents, whether in the nagging form of tough love or the gentle prodding of a supportive figure, has been underrated in its ability to lead to success. Even just the fact that as youngsters, we tend to avoid disappointing our elders, which is enough reason sometimes to keep pushing towards success.

Youthful Energy Will Aid Your Adventure

One problem we all have with obtaining specialized certificates is the fact that they require energy and are usually stressful. Being young, strong, and free meant that I could weather through each of the storms associated with studying and researching. There were many late nights spent reading everywhere, from the table, the couch, the floor, and even sometimes sitting in a half-filled bathtub (to ensure I didn't fall asleep). Someone once said that the glory of young ones is their strength, and I do agree.

Typically, it is the older individual who is working towards acquiring specialized certificates. Most of my older colleagues often had trouble going all the way, and some of them struggled with health issues and fatigue, and many times, their bodies would not be able to take the stress. As a younger student, our bodies can go as far as even surviving on noodles and fast food joints. Lack of sleep is usually the order of the week, and even then, I would have to wake early to make classes or meet appointments. If adults had to deal with a week of this, on the other hand, they would risk burnout. With the more energy I had from being younger, I could take more risks and do more than my older counter-parts, and being young meant that I could easily bounce back from any fatigue-related sickness.

You Get More Respect from People your Age

The moment you accomplish success in any venture, there is this posi-tive vibe or feeling you get, which gives a major boost to my self-esteem and pride. I would even confess this has built a bit of an ego in me too. Okay, maybe a lot. Nowadays, people do a double-take whenever they find out that I have more than one specialist certification. It is almost always a WOW moment for them, which precedes the questioning phase for me. Even more, it gets worse when I am around technology lovers and people with a little knowledge of computers. Parents, mentors, and guardians would also sometimes complicate matters as they would use me to boast at any chance they could get, whether at parties, family functions, or even in church meetings. They would start a discussion about me to someone else, and on it went. Others would use me as an object of comparison with their kids who they wanted to push into performing a task – sometimes, the responsibilities would be so innocuous, such as doing the dishes or taking out the trash. This style of discussion has gotten me into trouble time and time again, as more than one person has become angry at me because of it.

In conclusion, these are a few things I can quantify for what I have learned about getting a certification early in life. If you are still trying to decide whether or not to venture into getting a specialized certificate in any IT field, my advice is that you should.

Once you have decided on what career path you want to focus on, put all of your energy into it, and endeavor never to give up until you reach your goal. The younger you are, the better it may be for you too. Understand, all of the time and opportunities that you would have spent doing almost nothing could be invested in building your future and career.

If you consider yourself as not so young, this does not mean that you should give up self-improvement or career advancement. I don't believe it's ever too late to attempt another adventure or to follow a new path.

Whatever that goal is, whatever that achievement that you have always wanted to make, take the leap of faith, make a move, and do not ever doubt for once that you will succeed.

CHAPTER TWO
OBTAINING INTERNSHIPS EARLY

In the times of our parents, education was quite scarce among individuals in the labor market. However, with the developments in technology and the growth of social systems, education is now a necessity. Formerly, a university degree meant that you were guaranteed a well-paying job, a car, a house, and extreme prestige among your peers. Today, a different story is being told and experienced by our generation. University certificates are now so common among jobseekers that it no longer brings the edge and competitive advantage that it used to. Nowadays, employers ask for working experience, sometimes up to a year, if not more.

As a student about to graduate, I saw how hard it had been for my seniors and others before me to get a job in the very competitive labor market. Imagine my joy when I found that getting an internship would provide me with an edge after graduating. Interning also helped me accumulate real-world experience while continuing with my academics, and it introduced me to individuals that were important to my future, therefore enhancing my social network outreach. I was also lucky to earn a little cash on the side.

I don't think I can overemphasize the importance of gaining internships. These are some points that I learned while obtaining an internship:

Internships Provide Experience

The ability to observe and participate in the daily transactions of a firm will allow you to improve your knowledge and understanding of the theories that you have learned in school. Some scenarios are common in the business environment that are not discussed or mentioned during scholarly studies. Internships will help you follow up and test out new theories and ideas in IT sectors and ventures.

Internships Can Provide a Steady Income

Some firms and enterprises offer weekly or monthly stipends to interns. This makes their offers really tasty and increases the number of applicants that they get yearly. Also, the funds are usually very important to individuals, especially for students who are still in school, and they may help with transportation and feeding costs, while also helping in the development of your saving culture.

Internships Can Help Build a Meaningful Relationship

During internship programs, you'll have various opportunities to meet others who are in positions to help. Your talent, skill, and dedication will make sure that those who are above you notice you. The more you find and achieve bits of success, the more leadership will want to come in contact with you, either as mentors or friends. This is very important in setting you up for a better position and opportunity.

Internships Give You an Edge in the Labor Market

Even as the supply of university certified IT graduates become more than the demand of employers, there becomes a loss in value. Employers have to increase their criteria for hiring graduates, namely asking for experience. Having multiple internships can be a great way to let employers know that you have experience in a specific field and that they would not be hiring a green-hand, but rather an experienced individual who knows what they have to offer.

Firms that provide internship programs also equip students with valuable recommendations that will drastically improve the value employers put on the holders. In this case, the more, the merrier.

How to Gain Internships

Many institutions require that its students complete an internship program with businesses and enterprises that are related to it. This is designed to help students and scholars gain an understanding of everyday transactions and experiences associated with their chosen field of study. As mentioned above, interning with a firm would also give you experience that would make interns much more attractive to employers and provide them with an edge in the labor market.

More and more, students are now applying for multiple internships to improve their job-seeking advantage. Too, in this competition, you must know how to fish. Here are some tips I employed to grab available internship positions.

Volunteering

Not only in IT, but also in every other sector, there are organizations that accept volunteers, which helps you gain valuable work experience. Such opportunities usually come from non-profit organizations that are open to getting help and interested in helping to hone skills while also protecting you from error. Many students look down on volunteering because some of these organizations are usually not very popular and almost always never pay. Working conditions may also not be as conducive as we scholars would like or prefer, but as a young black woman, my strength is in my blood.

What many don't know is that apart from bringing you easy knowledge, you'll also have access to information to help you with experience and training. With those, you'll become much more knowledgeable in your chosen field of study. Volunteering can also bring you in contact with those who can help you find better positions and create opportunities in the future.

Networking

This is one of the most effective ways to make connections that could lead to getting not just any job, but one that you desire. Whenever you attend social functions, seminars, or workshops make it a culture to introduce yourselves politely to individuals you meet. All of the social graces and politeness are not for nothing, and you are likely to impress individuals who have information, position, or power, to land you that internship that will lead to a job opportunity.

To improve your reach and get yourself in front of the right audience, you should join affiliated student bodies and professional organizations that are related or based on the IT career path that you intend to pursue. You should make it a point to attend career fairs, networking events, and conferences, to get connected to the right people. Some online groups and platforms also facilitate building relationships and making connections with firms.

Do not forget that you could also make powerful connections at social functions, religious meetings, and even parties. Talk to your parents, friends, teachers, and mentors. Someone will know someone who knows someone else. Once you notice someone who has inside connections to a sector or firm that you have in mind, impress them and tell them about your goals and ambitions, and ask for their assistance. You may be surprised who you can meet in the most unsuspecting places.

Freelancing

Freelancing is a meaningful way to prove your value, skills, and capacity to prospective firms and employers. Many times, employers would prefer a physical evaluation and experience of your skill and ability before they give you an opportunity. Too, some of them have had unpleasant experiences with other interns, and with that, they would like to avoid a repeat, but they also do not have the time to test every applicant.

Strategies to Gain Internship

There are many tactics and approaches that can be employed to ensure that you have made the required preparations and that you are equipped to gain that post and position in a firm that you desire. Here are some of the few that have worked for me.

Early to Rise

In a very competent system, the early bird gets the best pick. Most of the desirable and popular enterprises and business owners usually start their internship programs early, and available spaces fill-up before the crowd arrives. It's important to begin your search earlier than others so that you get in before the applications start to clog the mailboxes.

Before public announcements are made, start reactivating your connections with alumni and internship bodies so that you can get the first pick of available options and positions. You'll want to get as much information as you can and run with it. Too, get your applications in long before deadlines are announced, and remember that you can always turn down or ignore any reply that is not to your liking as long as you have another option.

Know Your Interests

Many times, we hesitate and do things halfway because the opportunities and positions available to us are not the ones we want or desire. Having a goal and a list will help you to go after what you want and waste less energy on what you do not want. Your goals do not have to be overly specific so that you can have an abundance of positions and options to select. Make sure also to make a list of companies and firms that you want.

Also, having experience in different fields may not be a total waste as you can still build relationships and contacts, and the experience gained will improve your problem-solving skills and thinking capacity. Having an aim and a focus will help you maintain your drive and optimize your resources while searching for an internship.

Just Make the Call

Sometimes you have to reach out to the business owners, make the calls, send the application letters and, if possible, visit during working hours. Reach out to internship interests in your geographic location and inquire about offers and available positions in their firms. Prepare your pitch, an introduction of yourself, what you can do, and why they should want you. You may also find that agencies provide information on the needs of local employers and firms. Be sure to politely and firmly follow-up on firms and employers that you have spoken with, and always respect meetings and appointments that have been set up. Remember, whether or not you make the internship posts, you want to make a strong positive impression.

Start Your Own Business

If you are finding it hard to get an internship position, and you feel that time is running out, you may want to consider starting up a venture. Though this path is limited to those who have enough capital and funds, it is still respected and a valued form of gaining experience. You never know, you could also build something that would change lives, and you could meet customers and consumers who would link you with more prominent firms.

Be Prepared

To be prepared, do your research, and know what being an intern in a specific firm would mean. You'll need to ask relevant questions about the firm, such as, what does the firm make available for their interns and what is the length of the internship program. Be prepared to start at once, as sometimes a moment of indecision is all it takes to lose an important and invaluable opportunity. Too, be ready to convince firms and employers to take you on as an intern, and be prepared to offer yourself at a lower price or even for free. You should offer to be a company's first intern and prove your worth.

Persistent Follow-up

It is advised that you occasionally check in with the firms and employers to make sure that your letters have been received and not lost somewhere in the mix. You should send notes or make a call two weeks after you send in your application letter, and ask whether they want more information or inquire about more details. There may not be any positions available, but if one shows up, you have set yourself in the place to be remembered.

Work Hard

If you work hard, you set yourself up to be remembered positively, even after the end of your program. This means that apart from a favorable recommendation, those who have worked with you will have more than enough positive things to say about you as well.

I know you are already anxious to get into the pit and grab as many opportunities as you can, but also, you need to exercise patience. Internships are a form of examination by the employers to help them make the best hiring choices. There are some mistakes you don't want to commit when you have received a position, or you could potentially waste time and resources without understanding the full reward for your labors.

Below are a few:

- *Assumption and Hesitation*

  We are always subject to making assumptions about our bosses. One assumption is that our bosses know what we want and what we need without us communicating them. This is always the number one reason for missed opportunities and chances of getting jobs. You must approach your boss and explain your plans and purpose for interning with the firm. This will help establish a relationship and a path that will lead to you earning a job as well.

- *Ignoring Advice and Criticism*

  Sometimes we want the day to end as soon as it begins, so much so that we start to neglect our relationship with bosses and senior colleagues. You should ask for advice on how to improve yourself and present your work. This will show your dedication to your work and improve how employers and colleagues view you. Through this, you are sure to be given more responsibility, which will aid in reaching your goal.

- *Hiding*

  Many students are shy and lack a lot of social skills or confidence, which leads them to seek the dark corners of any group they find. Even when people have ideas that would put them in an advantageous position, the silence ensures they lose opportunities.

- *Unprofessional Behavior*

  Other students are not very disciplined and tend to be very obnoxious. This causes them to make jokes, use inappropriate language, and employ approaches that make their presence unwanted in the firm. These interns are usually kicked out before the end of the program, or they are ignored and given a bad recommendation if given one at all. It is essential to build your perception and understand the social system that you are in and how to interact appropriately in it.

- *Lacking Initiative*

  Ensure you don't sit in your cubicle after finishing the work that has been assigned to you. Don't be afraid and avoid more work, even if you bite off more than you can chew, and your boss will take note of your industriousness. When they do, you will improve the chances of landing a job opportunity, or at the very least, improve your chances of receiving a good recommendation and professional connection.

CHAPTER THREE
DIFFERENCES IN IT DEGREES

To most people (especially students), degrees in computer studies are so alike in their forms and course offerings that it is very tough to differentiate. The areas of study overlap, and sometimes practitioners can function little in the posts of one another.

It's essential to understand the differences and career paths that are available to holders and graduates of certificates in these fields of study. This will allow an individual to know precisely how to organize available resources to acquire what is desired. It is even more important to provide information to young and prospective professionals who desire a specific career path, but do not know what path to take to attain their goals.

There are three major areas or specific disciplines in the field of computer studies. They include Computer Engineering, Information Technology, and Computer Science. Career paths in these disciplines and areas are very different.

Computer Science

Computer science is much more involved in studying algorithms and advanced mathematical schemes that ensure the efficient and effective working of a computer system. Computer sciences are basically concerned with the operations of software, codes, and operating systems. Students of computer science study and research codes, learn different programming languages, various forms of advanced mathematics, and software design and development.

Computer science students are trained to understand the computer machine, the principles upon which they operate, and why they behave that way. This field relies entirely on mathematics to create programs and operating systems that perform the tasks we want.

Available Career Paths

- *Software Developer*

  This path requires a highly creative mind and intense problem-solving skills to create applications and program software, design systems, and build devices that are wanted and needed by the market. Software applications designed must be able to solve existing problems better than the software they may be replacing, while also being cheaper, more efficient, and optimized to better integrate with hardware components.

  Software developers are responsible for upgrades to existing software and application programs. They are also involved in the design and implementation of new and better-optimized software designs. This position is usually highly paid but is also typically based on the efficiency of the software created and the demand from the market.

- *Systems Engineer*

System engineers design and encode operating systems that run on computers, personal devices, cars, etc. Operating systems like Microsoft Windows, Linux, Android, and iOS are examples of operating systems. These operating systems are the basis for every other application system and are vital in making the application software integrate and work with available hardware. Too, the better the software, the more efficient is the performance of the hardware.

- *Web Developer*

Though web developers are very different from graphic designers, they are responsible for the images and outlook of websites. Web developers also program the code that makes a website behave the way it is programmed to perform. Web developers ensure that internet visitors can easily access and interact with the website and network user interface. They combine the visual graphics, audio and video, and also equip the site to monitor traffic, performance, efficiency, and functionality.

Computer Engineering

Computer engineers are studying and researching computer parts and how they work together. Computer engineers spend their time and resources designing and creating computer machine parts. A degree in computer engineering will equip you with knowledge and skills in building hardware such as circuit boards, video cards, and input hubs.

Computer engineering, like every other aspect of engineering, deals with the physical and electrical components of a computer system and how they work together to create a functioning system. Computer engineers have to create physical parts (or hardware) that can properly and efficiently integrate with the software and design, and components should be able to support a given program. For this reason, students of computer engineering are required to possess knowledge in both Computer Science and Information Technology.

Available Career Paths

Though career paths in the field of computer engineering are not as varied as in other fields, it is in no way inferior to the others. Also, they have positions in various industries where their services are essential and almost obligatory in the efficient running and development of their management and transactional processes.

- *Computer and Electronic Product Manufacturing*

  Most computer engineers work in this post, producing and manufacturing parts and products of computer hardware systems. Working in the factory, they ensure that products meet up with preset standards and specifications to ensure proper performance and safety of consumers.

- *Computer Systems Design*

  The computer systems design career path involves the design of requirements for the production of hardware and compatible software. It usually includes a bit of testing to produce hardware.

- *Scientific Research and Development*

  These posts are for those prepared to invest time in improving the efficiency and design of existing products. Newer products become available because of the activities and breakthroughs created by working researching engineers.

Information Technology (IT)

Information Technology (IT), also known as Information Systems or Systems Administration, studies are based on the usage and users of technology. IT uses current technology, hardware designs, and software in concert, to provide solutions to problems and issues of businesses and data management of institutions.

People who work in the IT department interact with clients and workers outside of their working environment. They help define innovative ways to understand and correct problems that challenge businesses, and they work with executives and business owners to design technological strategies that will help improve profit and solidify securities.

IT students are required to possess in-depth knowledge in the area of networks and networking, database design, and at least some knowledge in the basic and applied theories of mathematics. IT professionals require strong problem-solving skills and an innovative and creative mind. With every problem they come across, they must find a solution that is both efficient and cost-effective, using available resources.

Available Career Paths

Virtually every business institution requires the aid and services of an IT expert. From a low-level, small-medium enterprise down the street, to huge multinationals, IT professionals are a must-have for ensuring efficient business transactions.

- *Information Security Analyst*

   The more public a network becomes, the greater the potential of exposure to danger. Dangers may range from malicious software, like viruses and malware, to hackers and information thieves. The job of the Information Security Analyst is to protect the firm's data and network system, help prevent cyber-attacks, and consolidate weaknesses in cyber-securities. They also create backup plans and procedures to help firms survive the loss of data.

- *Network Architect*

   These are professionals in building and designing networks to enable computers to communicate and transfer data. Examples of such networks include local area networks (LAN), wide area networks (WAN), and an intranet. Network architects are also equipped to maintain and repair errors or problems that may occur.

- *Computer Support Specialist*

Computer Support Specialist professionals are equipped to provide advice and help individuals and businesses troubleshoot and solve problems or difficulties with software operation.

- *Database Administrator (DBA)*

Database Administrators engage applications and software to organize and store business transactional data that enables businesses to track and optimize their transactions.

- *Systems Administrator*

System Administrator professionals are involved in the day-to-day maintenance and operation of communication systems and networks that require the running of a business or institution.

So, there you have it, above are the ways to differentiate between the three disciplines of computer studies: Computer Engineering, Information Technology, and Computer Science. Hopefully, I have been able to make your choices and planning easier to complete. Now we go on to the timeline of certification available in the Information Technology discipline.

Degree programs in Information Technology help students gain an understanding of their chosen field of study and equip them for entry-level jobs. The bachelor's degree is designed to give students a foundational understanding, preparing them for higher-level and more specialized study programs.

Below are levels of degrees and certifications that a student may gain in a university.

Associate Degree in Information Technology

This level provides students with basic and foundational knowledge in the Information Technology discipline. The program is usually for a considerably short duration (two years) and requires students to get acquainted with basic technological concepts required. Course work includes website development, database administration, information systems, and of course, basic programming and programming languages.

Associate programs, depending on the institution, are sometimes focused on a particular area such as networking or securities, while other institutions take a broad path giving student knowledge in every possible area. Graduates of the associate degree programs are usually transferred into a higher institution for a bachelor's degree.

Bachelor's Degree in Information Technology

This degree provides a more comprehensive and in-depth study of computers and computing concepts. They are designed to equip the student with basic concepts and skills while increasing complexity from the first to the fourth year of the program. This program is usually offered by universities and enables students to dedicate themselves to specific areas of Information Technology, such as database management and security. Students are also required to take non-related courses, like environmental management and psychology, which would prove to be useful in real-world working situations.

Master's Degree in Information Technology

Master's programs are always very specific and designed to equip students in solving mostly higher-level problems that face companies and systems. This degree program enables students to gain jobs at the executive level and is designed to prepare students with leadership and management skills. The curriculum is set to allow students to study social and technological trends and set up systems that improve the efficiency and applications in business and social sectors.

Doctorate Degree in Information Technology

Popularly known as PhD, this degree is much more critical for students with very high aspirations in a very specialized and advanced sector. This program is designed to prepare students for research, teaching (in higher institutions), entrepreneurship, and others.

Students have to choose an area of concentration, such as management, digital forensics, cybernetic security, or software engineering. The program is usually very intensive and exhaustive in its approach, requiring students to acquire in-depth knowledge and skillset in a particular area. Ph.D. students are also required to formulate working hypotheses and research them, solve problems, and evaluate information and performance of IT systems, and, too, in the overall sector.

Graduates of the doctorate programs usually become integrated into the education system of universities and become professors, helping to prepare the next generation of IT professionals and improve the existing knowledge base. They also incorporate themselves into existing research institutes to help evaluate IT systems and theories that will enhance the efficiency of existing IT infrastructures.

Apart from the above degrees, there are also additional certificates that can help professionals broaden their skill range and improve the specialization in a specific area. Having any of these additional certifications can also enhance an individual's options and job opportunities. This is because some employers and firms may look for individuals with specific certificates, and due to the rarity of holders, these certificates can make a professional stand out in any group. These certificates may be applied for online or in physical institutions, offered in specific locations as part-time or full-time studies.

Cisco Certified Network Professional (CCNP)

To gain this certification, one must have been equipped and proved his skill and knowledge in running, maintaining, and troubleshooting various Cisco networks, especially voice, wireless, and security systems. Cisco certified professionals are globally recognized and very much respected in Information Technology societies.

Microsoft Certified Database Administrator (MCDA)

Microsoft provides individuals with study materials and globally recognized certification for professionals who want to specialize or increase their knowledge and skill in advanced Microsoft systems and software. Getting this certificate involves attaining a skill proficiency in creating, maintaining, and troubleshooting Microsoft databases.

Applied Certified System Administrator (ACSA)

Apple organizations also have certifications, and interested professionals must be prepared to prove their skills and knowledge in Apple's technical architecture and Mac operating systems. This ensures that certified professionals can find a place in businesses and infrastructures that employ Mac and Apple software designs to run their businesses.

CHAPTER FOUR
LEARNING THE POWER OF
NETWORKING EARLY

What is Networking?

Networking is a way of meeting new people, making new contacts, gaining more knowledge about specific skills, and building long-lasting relationships that could lead to more business-related benefits, such as ideas and information, as well as moral support.

Networking is not only useful socially, but it can also be applied to businesses, which will, in turn, benefit every member involved. Most relationships created from networking enable people to develop a new and more prominent platform for themselves with regard to opportunities, resources, and other new relationships that will emerge.

Networking also provides the opportunity to meet new people, open our minds and hearts to new ideas and perspectives, and learn new and different solutions to problems. It helps you create a connection with a large group of individuals with the same or closely related mindset, value, and interests. With time you will begin to gain each other's trust and then start to help each other whenever it may be needed. The more skillful, truthful, and trustworthy you are, to any member of your community, whenever you do business with them, the more your networking group will grow. Each connection will continue the progression of recommending you to other people, both internally and externally, to your group.

Early networking helps us learn from other people's success stories, while helping us to gain fresh ideas and see things from a new and different perspective. It gives you a head start about what to expect in your business as well, even as it grows. It makes you know what to expect at different stages and how to overcome various challenges as they show up. It can also help with meeting potential clients or gaining more job opportunities.

Networking should be a regular practice for both business owners and potential business owners (both small and large), and standard workers as well. Many jobs are achieved through recommendations or referrals, and with this in mind, everyone needs to develop a networking skill because it's indeed helpful in getting jobs or gaining clients. It's an essential way of building your brand and your business.

The more you pay attention and give time to networking, the more you gain knowledge about your business and other matters. It takes you a step ahead of others and allows you to know what is beneficial to you and your business. One of the most efficient methods to increase or expand your business is by creating a group with people who will be your cheerleaders. These are individuals that will make you and your skills, business, or ability, known and then move those individuals to recommend you for a job or business opportunity, which best suits your skills and abilities. Too, as they make recommendations, you will also move to recommend them as opportunities arise. Simply put, that is how networking works.

Networking is not an easy task because not everyone can stand talking to people for an extended period of time, or they may not be comfortable with meeting new people. However, it's something you must do if you want your business or skills to grow and be recognized. It requires full concentration and commitment, but at the same time, you don't always have to be the one doing the talking. There is so much more you can learn when you listen, and when it's your turn to add something to the discussion, you should say things that are worth listening to and are of interest.

Networking should be one of your utmost priorities. It will be an excellent advantage to you if you are actively involved in it. You should always add your point-of-view and perspective, whenever there is a group discussion, and make sure what you say counts. The best networking takes place when you don't know the title or influence of those with whom you are networking. Too, it's important to remember that most people don't like networking because they don't feel comfortable in environments that may feel intimidating, where you are forced to meet new people – especially those who may serve in roles of greater influence and power. So, to enjoy your networking group and discussions, you'd be best not to be too aware of your group member's social status, influence, or title, so as not to feel intimidated and lessen your confidence. Also, if you are already aware of their importance and power, don't let that weigh you down. You should still provide your perspective towards related subjects, because you may never know if what you have is the solution someone needs or is the answer to a situation.

Ultimately, your networking group may include anyone ranging from your colleagues at work, other business owners, friends, family, business connections, etc. Also, remember that not everyone knows how to network successfully. Written below are powerful tips on how you can network successfully.

Powerful Tips on How to Network Successfully

1. *Meeting new people through other people or at any function*

   You can't have successful networking in the comforts of your home, so you need to move out there in the world. You can decide to create new training, and/or attend functions and meetings, but you must know the types of new people you want to meet.

   Most times, people feel calmer and more relaxed at social gatherings, so meeting new people at functions helps you get a cool platform to discuss something without feeling tense. If you don't have any functions or meetings you need to attend as an opportunity to meet new people, you can surf online to know the locations of people with like minds, or you could attend fundraising functions and volunteer at events.

The fastest and easiest way to meet new people is through recommendations and referrals from other people you already know, so you need to maintain an excellent relationship with them. It's either they introduce you to them, or you contribute to discussions that will earn you a warm welcome. Then you can also tell them about yourself, your business, what you do, but don't make the whole conversation centered on you alone.

2. *Spend time social networking*

The social media platform is also a useful tool to know, meet, and potentially build a relationship with people of like minds, which proves to be positive when you don't have to think of what to say when you have an encounter with them physically. You can meet like-minded people on any social media platform, from Twitter to Instagram, and LinkedIn, by searching their profile or building your profile so well that it attracts like-minded people for you.

You can build a relationship with your like-minded connections by commenting or reacting to their online posts. This will help you begin a conversation with them online, while also building your confidence in preparation for meeting them physically. However, this doesn't mean that you should allow social media to consume your whole life or your time but have social media platforms aid in getting you what you want while also learning how to get more information about the people you want to meet.

Another way of networking on social media platforms is by posting or developing articles that your followers will find inspiring and educating, and also by answering questions and adding your own opinions and perspective during discussions, which will help build your brand.

3. *Networking is a two-way street, allow the other person to speak*

Networking is a two-way street, in which you should give the other person a chance to speak while you remember not to do all the talking. Don't let the conversations be centered on you alone. The best thing to do is to be an excellent listener. There is so much to learn if you can listen to people. If you are the one always doing the talking, it may shut them out because they will feel you are not interested in what they want to say or that you are not paying attention to what they want to share.

Whenever you meet new people, you must ask them questions about their business, the challenges they have faced, and how they have overcome. By doing so, you can, in turn, inform them about your business as well. To begin a conversation, you first start by asking basic questions such as, ask about their name, the name of their company or the company they work for, and the vision with which they are working. You may also ask other questions like:

- How long have you been in this business, or how long have you been working for the company?

- What do you like most or dislike about your business or job?

- What is your company's or business' mission statement?

- What products or services do you offer in your company or business?

- How do you compete with other rivals in the same field?

- What's is the difference between you and your competitors?

- Who are your clients or targeted audience?

- What challenges did you face over the years, and how did you overcome them?

As they answer you, make sure you listen and learn, and think of other questions you may want to ask them.

1. *Try your best to get a second meeting and build the relationship*

    Though the atmosphere of social gatherings may be relaxed and calm, meeting new people and introducing yourselves to new people can be a bit intense. Also, due to the time frame involved in social gatherings, you might not be able to obtain reliable information and details about the person. This is why it's important to request to meet with the person a second time. However, before you ask for a second meeting, make sure you try to determine if the relationship is worth it or if it will be of a great benefit to you and your business, and also if you can learn greatly from the person. If the relationship is not worth it or beneficial to you or your company, try and cut it short to move on, but do so politely.

To build a good relationship with other people, you must not let it stop at the first meeting. Create avenues for yourself if there are none, to tighten the bond already established. Here, you can send resources that can benefit them or their companies or businesses, and whenever opportunities that best suit their business or company arise, you can be sure to let them know.

2. *Be appreciative, always*

Networking is all about developing a natural, sincere, and long-lasting relationship. It's important to learn to appreciate people whenever anyone assists you or shares knowledge with you. Acknowledging people goes a long way in building a strong and efficient networking connection.

Benefits of Early Networking

Early networking has lots of beneficial effects on you and your business. It expands your thinking, visions, reasoning, and opportunities. As you build more room for more people in your networking group, you gain more recommendations and referrals, as well.

1. *Exchanging new ideas and knowledge*

No one is an island of knowledge, who stands alone. This is why we try to gain more experience and knowledge within and outside our field. Networking helps you learn direct knowledge and new ideas from other professionals in your field and from those who have gone far in your line of business. Networking is a high-quality medium through which you get more pieces of information, ideas, new views, and innovations that will help you grow in your field and aid in you gaining access to many things.

Gaining fresh ideas from other people in your networking group introduces you to various ways you can improve or enhance your business or company, which will make your business or company stand out amidst all the rest.

2. *It makes you gain a different perspective*

Even if you have acquired so much knowledge and information in your field, you still can't know everything about it. By meeting and interacting with other people who have gone ahead of you in your field, you will gain helpful insights and see things from a different view or new perspective. This will give you another way to see things, solve problems, and overcome challenges and circumstances involved in your business.

3. *It increases your visibility*

Gaining recognition, being visible, and standing tall amidst your competitors, your colleagues, and those in your field or industry should be a continuous practice. Networking helps in increasing your visibility because as you meet new people and they introduce or recommend you to other people, you begin to gain more popularity and recognition.

4. *It enhances your self-esteem and builds your confidence*

As you gradually meet new people and interact with them, you should question them to gain information, ideas, and perspectives, especially as you continue to boost your self-esteem and build your confidence. Networking also helps in building your social skills, especially if you are an introvert or very shy. Having strong self-esteem and confidence will help you interact effectively whenever you meet new people, and it will help you to create a long-lasting relationship with them.

5. *It helps build a long-lasting relationship*

Networking helps in building and developing strong and long-lasting professional and personal relationships that will move your company or your business forward, helping you to gain professional connections and take those to greater heights. Aside from professional information, you can also obtain personal advice that will make you an outstanding person. You should never take any introduction, recommendations, or referral, with levity. This is because you may never know which one will take you to a different horizon that you could have never imagined.

CHAPTER FIVE
ATTENDING IT CONFERENCES

Conferences are creative events organized to bring great and innovative minds together. Conferences also provide opportunities to discover great things, new strategies, new theories, and practical information. At conferences, you learn more about desired fields, and you have the opportunity to learn directly from field experts, within a short period of time.

Conferences are one of the greatest platforms to meet a large group of people in your field, physically. You can exchange ideas and perspectives, meet potential employers, employees, and clients, or you may potentially meet people who would like to work with you later in life.

Conferences usually involve you investing time, money, and energy as well, but at the end of it all, you will reap great benefits in multiple folds. If you don't want to be behind on innovation or creations in your field, then you need to attend conferences so that you gain access to fresh ideas and learn how to implement those ideas. Too, know that you are not wasting your time and energy, as you are taking time away from work, not for vacation, but in actuality, you are acquiring more knowledge and enhancing your career.

Conferences also add great value to you and increase your bank of knowledge. At conferences, you will learn how other people in your field manage to scale through some of the challenges they face in the industry, while also having the opportunity to showcase your handiworks and talents. To increase your visibility, you can also decide to volunteer to speak or present at conferences.

Everyone needs to attend IT conferences, whether you are a software engineer, quality assurance professional, system developer, security analyst, system administrator, etc. Attending conferences that are related, or closely related, to your field will help rekindle your love and zeal for your profession, learn ideas, and gain more knowledge from your colleagues, all while improving your profession.

Essentially, attending conferences with people of like minds makes you feel like you are in an intellectual gathering where you can meet with people and have an opportunity to discuss new research, projects, and also, new developments. Conferences are sources of inspiration to all attendees as well, because it creates an avenue for you to meet people, get fresh ideas, and increase visibility, though sometimes the experiences can be daunting and overwhelming.

There are lots of reasons why you need to attend IT conferences, and written below are a few reasons why.

Why Do You Need to Attend IT Conferences

1. *You will learn new things*

   Though you can access loads of ideas and knowledge online, it'll never be the same as attending a conference. You will learn new things and get ideas not only from the speakers at the conference, but also from the new people you meet at the events. Too, you'll have the opportunity to review and learn about the latest techniques and innovations in your field.

2. *You will have lots of fun*

   "All work and no play makes Jack a dull boy."

   Not all conferences are dull, though, in the past, some have assumed otherwise. You can spice things up yourself, too. For example, you can talk and share with other people to hear their views and perspectives about the things you've seen or learn from the conferences. You can take a tour around the vicinity of the event, or grab a drink with some of the attendees of the conference.

3. *You will gain more knowledge and inspiration*

   You will gain more knowledge and inspiration right from the beginning of a conference and until the very end. This may come from speakers, experts in your field, and from those you meet at the conference. Too, they will potentially stir in you lots of zeal and motivation to do more great things in your profession.

4. *You will have access to many opportunities*

At a conference, you can connect to potential clients, employers, or employees, and also get to learn about various job opportunities.

Tips on How to Get the Most Out of Conferences

To help you develop and establish a foundation for you to be able to have a successful conference experience, written below are various things you can do.

Once you get to the conference, you can find a professional friend in your field who will act as your friend and supporter, throughout the conference. After each session, you both can sit and share everything you've learned. This will make you see another perspective on what was shared and what you gained during each session. Too, these relationships created can continue, even after the events of the conference.

You should go through the conference timetable to check and choose the sessions that will benefit you, as well as those that will sharpen and improve your skills. Next, attend meetings where you will learn something new or attend meetings that will prove and expound upon your existing knowledge.

Be sure to ask questions and comment on topics, as the opportunity arises to do so. Also, don't be late for any session or leave the conference hall before the session's end time. If you were to do so, you could miss out on some vital information or opportunities.

Never isolate yourself from the rest of the attendees, and make it a point to meet with new people and expand your networking group. There are opportunities everywhere, and you can't find them if you sit in one place. As you meet people, make sure you collect their business cards and share yours with them as well, and when you receive a card, don't dispose of them but use them to follow-up with the individual, wither by giving them a call or sending them an SMS or email. Be sure always to be appreciative, as it will draw people closer to you.

Finding the Right Conference to Attend

Not all conferences are worth attending, so you need to perform thorough research about any conference you want to participate in so as not to waste your time, energy, and your money.

Here are three things you must consider when choosing the right conference.

1. *Who are the organizers?*

   Before you make up your mind to attend any conference, make sure you research thoroughly about the business or career that it is targeting and also check through the website of the conference host. The information you need about the conference will be provided on the conference website, and if you are not satisfied with what you read and see, don't attend.

2. *Where is the conference holding?*

How safe is the environment or vicinity where the conference will be held, and ask yourself, will it be safe enough to take a walk or tour in the city, and overall, will you be safe there? These are essential questions you need to answer, concerning the location of the conference, before you decide on going. Make sure to choose a location where it will be safe enough to go out for a drink with friends or take a tour around the city.

3. *Go through the conference timeline*

You already have your expectations for the conference you want to attend, so, as not to get your hope smashed, you need to go through the conference timeline. The timeline will act as a guide to know if you will be able to acquire that skill or knowledge you seek, and it will provide information on the speakers and the duration of each session. If you are pleased with the timeline, then you should look positively at attending the conference.

Benefits of Attending IT Conferences

1. *You get to meet face-to-face with professionals*

   Online conferences do not give you the chance to meet with professionals physically, but attending conferences allows you to meet face-to-face with the professionals in your field, with those you've always looked up to and those you admire. Here, you can have the opportunity to have a chit chat, ask them questions, or take a selfie with them, which may lead to having a relationship with them as well.

2. *You will have the energy and zeal of like-minded colleagues*

   Being in an environment where everyone is passionate and enthusiastic about the same thing will make them do and feel great and could potentially help them to better themselves. Meeting and talking with like minds will stir up a zeal in you to do the impossible, do things that have never been done before in that field, and will make you want to improve your skills and acquire more knowledge. Online conferences cannot match up to this.

3. *It enhances networking*

   There is no doubt that you can have access to anyone you want to gain access to on social media. No matter where the person might be in this world, nothing can compare to meeting and talking with the person face-to-face, which allows you the opportunity to see their emotions, physically. It's no wonder they say, "our actions speak louder than our voice."

Not all talks and discussions can be fully understood if they are on social media, whereas face-to-face conferences create a platform where you can meet with the right people, in a physical environment. For instance, potential mentors, clients, employers, or employees, will be present, and this allows you to make yourself known and visible, and it allows you the opportunity to potentially develop a relationship with them, by spending most of your free time with them.

4. *It helps you to break out of your comfort zone*

Attending conferences enables you to break out of your comfort zone, and it makes you stretch yourself to others and opportunities. With this, things you may typically find challenging, and probably won't do on the norm, could have a chance to be better. They'll make you try new things, visit new places, and perhaps also, change your mindset, view, or perspective.

5. *It sharpens the saw*

Imagine you have a tree you want to cut, and you have an ax in your hand but can't cut the tree the way you want. This would show that you have to find a better option that will help to cut the tree the way you are wanting. At conferences, you gather more information, learn new approaches, and target innovation. As you know, technology advances daily, so thinking of fresh ideas and developing innovations may too revolve daily. In this, it's important to attend conferences that will help to inspire you and make you gather adequate knowledge on how to best cut that tree.

6. *It helps you to have lots of fun*

Apart from going to a conference where you will learn more, while also having access to many series of discussions and talks from the speakers, you can also have lots of fun by meeting lots of people. With those people, you will get an opportunity to talk about exciting things, and you can take time to plan to explore the city with your new friends as well.

Most conferences understand this as an attractive component to the conference and have side events on their timeline, such as offerings of dinner parties, meet-and-greets, or networking opportunities, and they provide fun receptions as well. So, who says you can't have lots of fun as you learn great new things? Be sure to enjoy your conference to the fullest.

7. *It comes with a package or takeaway*

Like I said earlier, attending conferences is like making an investment. You'll invest your precious time, energy, and, most importantly, your money or company's money, for as we know, attending conferences can be costly. Despite this, you know that you will surely reap a fruitful harvest from attending. For instance, during the conference, you get to ask direct questions from the speakers or professionals, you'll have opportunities and inspirations that arise, networking opportunities will be made available, new approaches, skills, ideas, and innovations will be learned about and gained, and most importantly, you'll have a wonderful experience that improves yourself, widens your knowledge base, your business, career, or company, and you'll gain more insight as you learn.

These are the packages you get from attending conferences, and no one can take them away from you.

8. *Have the opportunity to learn new things in your field and beyond*

Aside from gaining knowledge, learning to further innovation, and gaining ideas about your field, at conferences, you can also learn things that are external to your field. Essentially, no knowledge is lost, and what you learn today can never be taken away from you. Learning new things that are outside your field helps you take a step ahead of others. What you learn today may be needed tomorrow, as you never know the future, and once you've acquired that new knowledge, it's there forever.

With everything you have gained from this chapter, I hope you apply them whenever you have the opportunity to attend an IT conference. Remember, don't look at the time you will spend there or the amount of money that it will take to cover all your expenses or the energy it will require. Simply set your gaze on that package, that great fruitful harvest you will reap once you invest, and then the sky will be your starting point.

CHAPTER SIX
LEARNING TO BE PUBLISHED IN
IT JOURNALS

Writing journals and getting those published in IT journals is indeed a blessing, but not everyone in the IT or engineering fields will get their journals published. This is because they may start the process on the very wrong track, or they are in a hurry to get it published, so they miss a step.

Getting your journals published in IT journals can be very productive. Publications brings recognition, certificates, awards, speaking tours, and popularity, but that also requires a lot of patience, energy, knowledge, and time. It's not something that happens overnight.

For those in the IT industry, it's almost everyone's dream to have their works published in IT journals.

What are Journals?

Journals are scholarly or academic publications that contain articles that are written by professionals, lecturers, researchers, and experts. Journals are written periodically, and focus on a particular discipline or field of study. Too, journals are not available for everyone to read, because they are used for presentations and mostly for the discussion of research.

Journals enable lecturers, professionals, and researchers to make available the processes and results of their research on various topics, that ranges from fundamental topics to comprehensive topics. Journals serve as a guideline to help other researchers who are ready to make their research known, and too, to establish connections to previous works published in the past.

Journals also help in improving your research profile and the progression of your career in your specific discipline. They serve as an avenue to learn from the people who have already gone ahead of you in research and the publication of journals.

To make our world better and to make sure our technology keeps advancing and improving, we have to acquire knowledge continuously. It's vital to gain knowledge, and then try to conduct high-quality research that will help develop, expand, and enhance the scientific and technological aspects of our lives.

Researchers define a one of a kind hypothesis, acquire data, and employ the methodology of the research. The purpose of the journal is to provide theoretical knowledge by sharing the theoretical and practical implications of the research performed. After they complete their research and the compilation of theoretical aspects, they then submit the manuscript for publication in a peer-reviewed journal.

Many researchers who want their works to be published often face difficult challenges when it comes to manuscript preparation, compilation, and the submission of journals. Any mistakes made at this stage can lead to the research being rejected for publication, therefore, it's better to avoid errors to get your manuscript published.

Writing scholarly journals can be very competitive due to the recognition and career progression it offers. Anything could cause your work to be rejected, and it is understood that you can't see all the mistakes in your manuscript, which is why your work must pass through the journal peer-review processes. This is an important step because it's an important part of any publication process.

For anyone who wants to have their works published in IT journals and does not want their works to be rejected due to some mistakes, written below are some helpful tips that will assist you in preparing and compiling your manuscripts, with either qualitative or quantitative methodologies, for the information technology and engineering disciplines. They include:

1. *Never be in a hurry to submit your manuscript for publication*

    As a scholar or professional, you don't have to be in a hurry to get your work published. Instead, you should start by writing articles for information technology, engineering, or science magazines, which will help improve your writing skills.

    After compiling your manuscript, you don't have to submit it once you are done with your conclusion. However, some authors believe that they will still have the chance of correcting all their mistakes once they have received the manuscript back from the journal editor and the reviewers who will help identify errors.

By acting in advance, before submission, you can help decrease the chances of getting disappointed from feedback received or from having your work rejected. You need to ensure you follow activities that will help you have a well-prepared manuscript. The activities include:

- Subsequent reading of your manuscript, which will help you see the errors and mistakes within your manuscript.
- Give your manuscript to your colleagues and other researchers in your field and ask them for feedback.
- These activities will help prevent disappointment and rejection.

2. *Choose a suitable publication outlet*

Submitting your manuscripts to the right publication outlet that perfectly suits your research and discipline will help enhance your chances of getting your manuscript accepted, and it will ensure its made available to your target audience.

Research policies and ethics suggest that manuscripts should be submitted to only one journal publication outlet at a time. This is because it can be very implicating, while causing considerable damage, should you try submitting your manuscript to different publication outlets simultaneously.

3. *Carefully go through the aims, objectives, and author's guidelines of your selected publication outlet.*

After you have carefully read your manuscript, shared your manuscript with your colleagues, received feedback on your manuscript, and after you have chosen a publication outlet, then you will want to carefully go through the aims and objectives of the journals in your specific research field. Download and read the author's guidelines and make sure your manuscript abides by the guidelines and requirements, as it's essential to ensure your manuscript follows the requirements and guidelines of your selected publication outlet to avoid the rejection of your manuscript. Too, some journal publishers reported that one manuscript out of five does not follow the required layout, style, and format of the publication outlet, which leads to rejection. If the outlet is not pleased with your manuscript, they will move to reject your manuscript, and rejection or disappointment can be saddening and disheartening for the authors of those manuscripts.

4. *Have a captivating title and abstract*

Your title and your abstract are the most crucial components of a manuscript. You need to make those components captivating so that they prompt the journal editors to be more interested in your manuscript. Seeing a captivating title and abstract will make the peer-reviewers or journal editors, and anyone else who goes through your manuscript, have a good feeling towards your manuscript.

Too, remember, you know that "first impression count."

5. *Consult a professional editing company to help you proofread and make the necessary editing of your manuscript.*

In order to have a better manuscript to submit to the publication outlet, it's better to reach out to a professional editing company that will help you to copy-edit your manuscript. This will include editing of the list of references, tables, figures, and the main body text, because one of the essential characteristics of writing for any journal is clarity. Many journals have been rejected due to the poor construction of sentences and language. The services rendered by the copy-edit company is irrefutable.

When you submit a well-written, error-free, properly copy-edited, understandable, and well-constructed manuscript for publishing, your manuscript will stand a better chance of been published. This process will also make the editorial board go through your manuscript more carefully. Also, be sure to proofread your manuscript yourself for efficiency accuracy and avoid wordy sentences. However, not everyone can afford the services of a professional copy-editing company, so if you fall into this category, you've got nothing to worry about because some applications or websites are available, which will scrutinize spellings, grammar, and mechanics. Some examples are Grammarly and Microsoft Word, etc. With those applications, you can submit your manuscript to make available proper editing checks.

6. *Add a cover letter with the manuscript whenever you want to submit it.*

Never underestimate the importance of a cover letter addressed to the editor, or editor-in-chief, of the target journal. Last year, I attended a conference in Boston. A "meet the editors" session revealed that many submissions do not include a cover letter. The editors-in-chief present, who represented renewed and ISI-indexed Elsevier journals, argued that the cover letter gives authors a vital opportunity to convince them that their research work is worth reviewing.

There is this grace that comes with the cover letter you submit with your manuscript, and not everyone knows this fact. Whenever you want to submit your manuscript, add a cover letter that is addressed to the editor-in-chief of the selected journal. This will help in proving to them that your research deserves to be reviewed.

In this, be sure to write the cover letter carefully, don't be in a hurry when writing it, and know that you don't have to put your research abstract in the letter because, essentially, it's useless. An excellent cover letter should entail:

- Outlines of the main topic of your research.
- Discuss the innovation of the research.
- Explain the significance of your manuscript to the selected journal.
- Acknowledged everyone who helped you in reading the manuscript and those who gave you feedback in the cover letter, but ensure that you don't write a wordy cover letter and keep it to half a page, preferably.

7. *Pay adequate and careful attention to the reviewers' comments*

Usually, the editors, or editors-in-chief, depend on the total acceptance of manuscripts based on the recommendations given by the reviewers, especially if the recommendation is written to "revise and resubmit." Comments made by the reviewers should be properly or carefully attended to because any changes made in the manuscript can either cause damages or make your work more perfected. Too, the revisions stated by the reviewers might require either a large or small change in the manuscript, which is why you need to successfully take the steps involved in the revision process, which includes:

Step one: Once you've received the manuscript, attend to the revisions carefully.

Step two: Pay close attention to all the comments and avoid omitting any comments received.

Step three: Ensure you submit the revised manuscript before the deadline given by the selected journal.

Step four: Complete the revision processes, and do so with the submission of two required documents, which are:

- The initial manuscript that the reviewers highlighted with corrections and the recommendations you need to apply.
- The second document should be in the form of a letter that entails your feedback that clarifies that you have carefully addressed the corrections made by the reviewers or the editors.

Make sure these two documents are properly written and formatted. You are free to concur or dissent the reviewers or editors' comments. Still, it is better to agree with their comments, especially since if you decide to not coincide with the editors' comments, you must then provide substantial evidence that will justify your action.

Following these revision processes is not difficult, though it may appear to be challenging to carry out. Following these steps will help you pay proper attention to the reviewer's recommendations and comments, and the process will increase the chances of getting your work published.

In conclusion, I know that having your work published in the journal of your choice is like a stepping stone for you to be well recognized, rewarded, and productive, but if your work is rejected, you don't have to be sad or lose hope. In such a case, you should try another attempt at research and submission, and try to avoid the same mistakes that resulted in the previous rejection. Ensure you follow the right steps, and only then will your manuscript be accepted in the journal of your choice, and following, you will surely be on your way to greatness.

Also, don't forget to keep trying again, and again, and again, as you may never know when the sun will shine on you.

You can also try talking to the professionals in your field who have gone ahead of you, so that they may guide and direct you on how to successfully get your work published in journals.

CHAPTER SEVEN
LEARNING THE BENEFITS OF BEING AN ENTREPRENEUR

With understanding the difference between Small Business Owner and Running A Small Business

This chapter is in two phases, the first phase will discuss the benefits of being an Entrepreneur, and the second phase will discuss the difference between small business owners and running a small business.

Who is an Entrepreneur?

An entrepreneur is someone who develops, organizes, directs, or operates one or more businesses. Generally, they are risk-takers, who are passionate and confident, creative and determined, problem identifiers and problem solvers, opportunists, and innovative individuals.

Entrepreneurs are like a foundation in which other platforms are built. They continually try their best to ensure that their actions and fruit improve venture growth, the economy, and the development of the company.

Entrepreneurs are a unique set of individuals because they think about how to solve problems faced and about how to bring their ideas and visions to life. Some enter into entrepreneurship for the passion they have towards it, while some become entrepreneurs because of the high income that potentially could be achieved.

Entrepreneurship isn't a child's play, as it's perpetually demanding, the venture faces enormous challenges, and it creates considerable risks. Entrepreneurship is not meant for everyone either, and it must be remembered that this venture strongly involves the implementations of ideas. Entrepreneurs take every problem they see around them, and they see themselves as a chance to develop a product or service that will serve as a solution to the problem.

Before you can be a successful entrepreneur, you must first identify a problem, have an idea on how to solve the problem, create a vision, and then become passionate about transforming that vision into a business. You must then be able to have access to necessary information, resources, and networking, that will help you to be a successful entrepreneur. For example, commitment, awesome ideas, and passion are some of the characteristics you will need to become an entrepreneur. When you are joyful doing what you love doing, you won't see the challenges or obstacles involved. Instead, you will see yourself overcoming.

Aside from being able to do what you are passionate about, I'm so pleased to tell you that the benefits of being an entrepreneur are incredibly rewarding.

Benefits of Being an Entrepreneur

1. *You get to have your own schedule*

    One of the advantages of being an entrepreneur is that you get
    to choose your working hours and not follow the regular work-
    ing hours. Developing a successful business can be demanding,
    which can require more time, but you have the freedom to decide
    when you would like to work. This makes you have time for
    other things in your life by not spending a whole lot of time sit-
    ting in your office.

2. *You are always in charge*

    Entrepreneurship enables you to be the primary driver of your
    company. You get to do work with your ideas and visions, build
    a team with like-minded individuals, make every decision about
    the affairs, growth, and development of the company, permitting
    you to be in charge of everything.

3. *You gain full leadership experience*

    Being an entrepreneur will help build up your leadership skills
    by making you more conscious of time and commitments. It
    will also develop characteristics, such as becoming more fo-
    cused, self -disciplined, calm, optimistic, passionate, and bold,
    all while improving your social skills. Even outside of the four
    walls of your company, these traits would still be imbibed in

you, and those will reflect on whatever you do, wherever you are.

4. *Freedom to work anywhere you choose*

You are free to create your own working space. Entrepreneurship enables you to work anywhere, provided that you can get access to the Internet. You can work wherever you so desire, like your home, parks, bars, restaurants, or inside your car, instead of an office, which may enable you to do other things while working. It's not a must for you to work inside an office.

5. *Constant growth and development*

With the leadership skills you have acquired over time, it helps you in doing all you can to see that your company grows continuously, while also ensuring that you focus on the development of your company, as your main priority.

6. *You have a total freedom*

Entrepreneurs have the freedom to do what they please with their company, and rules do not bond them. They are free to do anything that will undoubtedly lead to the growth and development of their company. They are the potter, and their company is the clay, so they can mold it into any shape they like, so far as it will be beautiful, profitable.

7. *It increases your self-confidence*

Some obstacles or challenges faced by entrepreneurs can prove very tough and can be challenging to overcome, but once you learn to overcome challenges, you'll know your abilities. You must believe strongly in yourself, and do what you know you can do, and then no problem will look difficult to you because your self-confidence will keep increasing, constantly.

8. *You get to reap the whole harvest*

Every recognition, compliment, award, or profit belongs to the entrepreneur because you were the one who sowed your all into your company, so everything you get from it belongs to you. No one else will claim your success or reap the harvest of your labors.

9. *You will feel fulfilled*

Once everything is in place, and your visions and ideas are brought to life, you will see that you are fulfilling the purpose for which it was all created. There is joy that will fill your heart, and the feeling of can't stop.

How would you feel if you see that your sleepless nights, the energy you put into your company, and the many challenges that you faced, resulted in you providing solutions to humanity through your products or services? I'm sure the feeling will be inexpressible.

10. There's no limit to your earnings

As an entrepreneur, there is no limit to the amount of money you earn daily, weekly, or monthly. Your profits are the rewards of your energy, ideas, hard work, and commitments. Should you like, you can increase your source of income. Thus, it indeed pays to be an entrepreneur.

Are you thinking what I'm thinking? Why not look around your community, environment, country, or the world, and see the kind of problems humanity is facing. You may then begin to think of a solution to the problem, and remember to be passionate and focus on bringing those ideas to life, and then you will surely be on the path of being a successful entrepreneur.

Now that you've learned about entrepreneurs and the benefits of being an entrepreneur, let's discuss the difference between small business owners and running a small business because not every-one is conversant with those differences.

Small Business Owners

Some people refer to small business owners as solo entrepreneurs. Small business owners are local company owners with a small number of em-ployees. Small business owners create job opportunities for the people in their community and also help in developing the community. Small businesses built in local communities help in expanding the commercial economy of the community. Too, most times, that will be where most youths get their first jobs as well. Without these small business owners, our economy could dwindle.

Small businesses are independently owned companies, and they are operated mostly in local communities, having employees at numbers that are less than 500. Small business owners have the ideas to rebrand existing products or services, thereby creating job opportunities, and they have two priorities, to serve and give back to local communities and to earn a living for themselves.

There are lots of traits or characteristics that best describe successful small business owners or solo entrepreneurs. Written below are some of the characteristics you will see in them.

1. *They are powerfully driven*

   They are highly determined to be successful, and they are always after the growth of their company, right from its foundation to then becoming a fully established company. Despite the challenges and the difficulties they will face, they are strongly determined and more motivated to see their company grow continuously.

2. *They are passionate*

   When you are not passionately in love with what you do, then you are bound to fail. Being passionate about your company will make you do all you can to make it a success-ful one. Small business owners are always passionately in love with what they do because they will still go the extra mile to make their company better.

3. *They embrace teamwork*

They don't do everything alone, and they delegate work tasks or duties to employees and other people in the organ-ization, which helps running the company go more smoothly and creates a better pathway to success. They also focus on developing a lasting relationship with everyone on the team, as each contributes towards the development and success of the company. Such members that engage team-work, for instance, will be their employees, clients, etc.

4. *They are humble*

Small business owners are not pompous or too proud to ask anyone for help when they need it, or to accept faults and corrections. Even after being successful in getting the com-pliments and awards of being a small business owner, they remain humble. They are appreciative of everyone that con-tributes to the success of the company because they don't take all the glory. They also never despise the days of their small beginnings.

5. *They are always inquisitive*

Small business owners are not always satisfied with their ideas or results thereof, because they keep the mindset of continual rebranding concerning their existing ideas and their consequences. This is why they are always looking for ways to improve and expand their company, improve their products or services, retain their employees, get more clients, and stay ahead of their competitors.

6. *They possess self-confidence*

They are always confident in themselves, with whatever they do and with their ideas, because they are mainly responsible for the success of their company. They believe in themselves and the things they do because they are sure it will lead to victory.

7. *They are time conscious*

Being time conscious is one of the keys and an active ingredient in making your business grow continually. Small business owners are time managers, and they work according to their plans and schedules established for a specific day. Since they delegate duties to other people in their company, they will have time to concentrate on other things.

Planning your day and working by its schedule makes your day more fruitful.

Running a Small Business

Running a small business is not a child's play, and it takes more than just diligence and hard work. Not everyone can successfully run a small business because not everyone is conversant with the basic knowledge of running a small business. Running a small business requires having full knowledge of how to run a small company, how to build good relationships with employees and clients, and, throughout, requires that you know how to present your goods and services pleasantly. You must also have a good and reliable business plan that will help run the small business successfully.

Running a small business involves adequate preparations and effective planning that will help handle challenges that may be faced, like finances issues, employee issues, and client or customer issues, that may arise later. Planning is also essential in that it will help promote the company and further the company's constant growth. Though running a small business can be very challenging, there is a great reward attached to being successful, because a successful small business will be beneficial to the owner, employees, customers, and also the local community.

Running small businesses is not for timid people. In order to successfully run a small business, there are essential steps that you need to follow, and they include:

Step one: Draft a good business plan

The first step you to take in order to run a successful business is to have a business plan. It's imperative to write down your vision, goals, reasons for starting the company, and ideas you have to ensure success. This serves as a guideline for you whenever you want to make decisions that are related to your business.

Step two: Capital

Running a small business requires having a substantial financial resource. You need to have sufficient capital so that the company will keep running before you start generating revenue, and before you begin to earn income, profit, and revenue. You also will have to plan to spend on the operational costs of the company. Too, you must know the cost of producing your products and services and know how much your income will be before you start running your small business.

Step three: Develop good team members

Running a successful small business requires gathering and developing high-quality team members that will help contribute to the success of the company, for example, your employees. You must gather high-quality team members that are ready to make sure that the business goes forward smoothly and effectively.

Step Four: Develop an effective marketing strategy

Developing a marketing strategy is very important when it comes to running a small business because marketing strategies are how you attract more customers to patronize you. You need to focus on developing an effective marketing strategy that will attract and retain your desired target audience.

Step Five: Identifying your customer base

You need to be sure you know your target audience. You must identify those that will buy your products or services and then be sure that your goods and services meet the needs of those within your target audience and even those living within the local community, to build a strong customer base.

Step Six: Confidence

Confidence is perhaps the most essential characteristic of a small business owner. As it is often said, no one will believe in you if you do not believe in yourself. Customers prefer to do business with professionals who appear competent and secure in their abilities.

Step Seven: Believe in yourself

No one else can understand your vision and ideas more than you, so you need to believe in yourself, your ideas, and your insights. Don't forget to project confidence to everyone around you.

Made in the USA
Columbia, SC
04 June 2020